PUSH AND PULL!
LEARN ABOUT MAGNETS

BY JULIA VOGEL

The Child's World®

Published by The Child's World®
1980 Lookout Drive • Mankato, MN 56003-1705
800-599-READ • www.childsworld.com

ACKNOWLEDGMENTS
The Child's World®: Mary Berendes, Publishing Director
Content Consultant: Paul Ohmann, PhD, Associate Professor of Physics,
      University of St. Thomas
The Design Lab: Design and production
Red Line Editorial: Editorial direction

PHOTO CREDITS: Awe Inspiring Images/Fotolia, cover, 1, 2, 3, 4, 6, 8, 10, 12, 14, 16,
18, 20, 22; Michael Chamberlin/Fotolia, 5; Kathy Libby/Fotolia, 6; Fotolia, 7, 19 (bottom);
Christy Thompson/Fotolia, 9 (top); Michael Flippo/Fotolia, 9 (bottom); Andrea Church/
Fotolia, 11; Jane Yamada, 13, 23; Izaokas Sapiro/Fotolia, 15; April Cat/Fotolia, 17;
Oleksandr Moroz/Fotolia, 19 (top); Dave Riganelli/Fotolia, 20; Jason Stitt/Fotolia, 21

LIBRARY OF CONGRESS CATALOGING-IN-PUBLICATION DATA
Vogel, Julia.
  Push and pull! Learn about magnets / by Julia Vogel ; illustrated by Jane Yamada.
    p. cm.
  ISBN 978-1-60253-513-8 (lib. bd. : alk. paper)
  1. Magnetism—Juvenile literature. 2. Magnets—Juvenile literature. I. Yamada, Jane, ill.
II. Title.
  QC757.5.V64 2010
  538—dc22   2010010981

Printed in the United States of America in Mankato, Minnesota.
July 2010
F11538

CONTENTS

A Mysterious Force

You can't see it.
You can't hear it.
But it has the power to push and pull.
It's inside Earth.
It's everywhere around your home.

What is this mysterious force?
It's the power of magnets!

The force of the magnet holds these little screws tight. ▶

Will It Stick?

You know that magnets stick to the fridge. Why? The door has a thin colored coating. But underneath, there's metal.

Magnets **attract** certain kinds of metal. Most often, magnets stick to iron. They can also pull on other magnets.

Nails have a lot of iron. Would they stick to magnets? ▶

A pair of scissors, a thimble, and a needle would stick to magnets. The thread and the wooden spool would not. ◀

Pennies don't scoot to a magnet.
Neither does gold.
Paper and pencils stay put, too.
These things are not made of iron.
They are not **magnetic**.

Coins are the wrong type of metal for sticking to magnets. ▶

Pencils, paper, and things made of plastic do not stick to magnets. ▶

8

Magnets come in different sizes and shapes. Which one can pick up the most stuff? It may not be the biggest one!

Even small magnets can grab things they're not touching. Hold a refrigerator magnet above a paper clip. You can make the paper clip jump!

Magnets can be round. They can be rectangles or look like horseshoes. ▶

But what happens if you move the paper clip across the room? The trick doesn't work.

Around each magnet is an invisible space. This space is called its **magnetic field**. A magnet works only inside its magnetic field.

Scientists imagine a magnetic field as lines that loop from one end of a magnet to another. Try putting a piece of paper over a magnet. Then sprinkle the paper with small pieces of iron. The pieces will move into lines like these. ▶

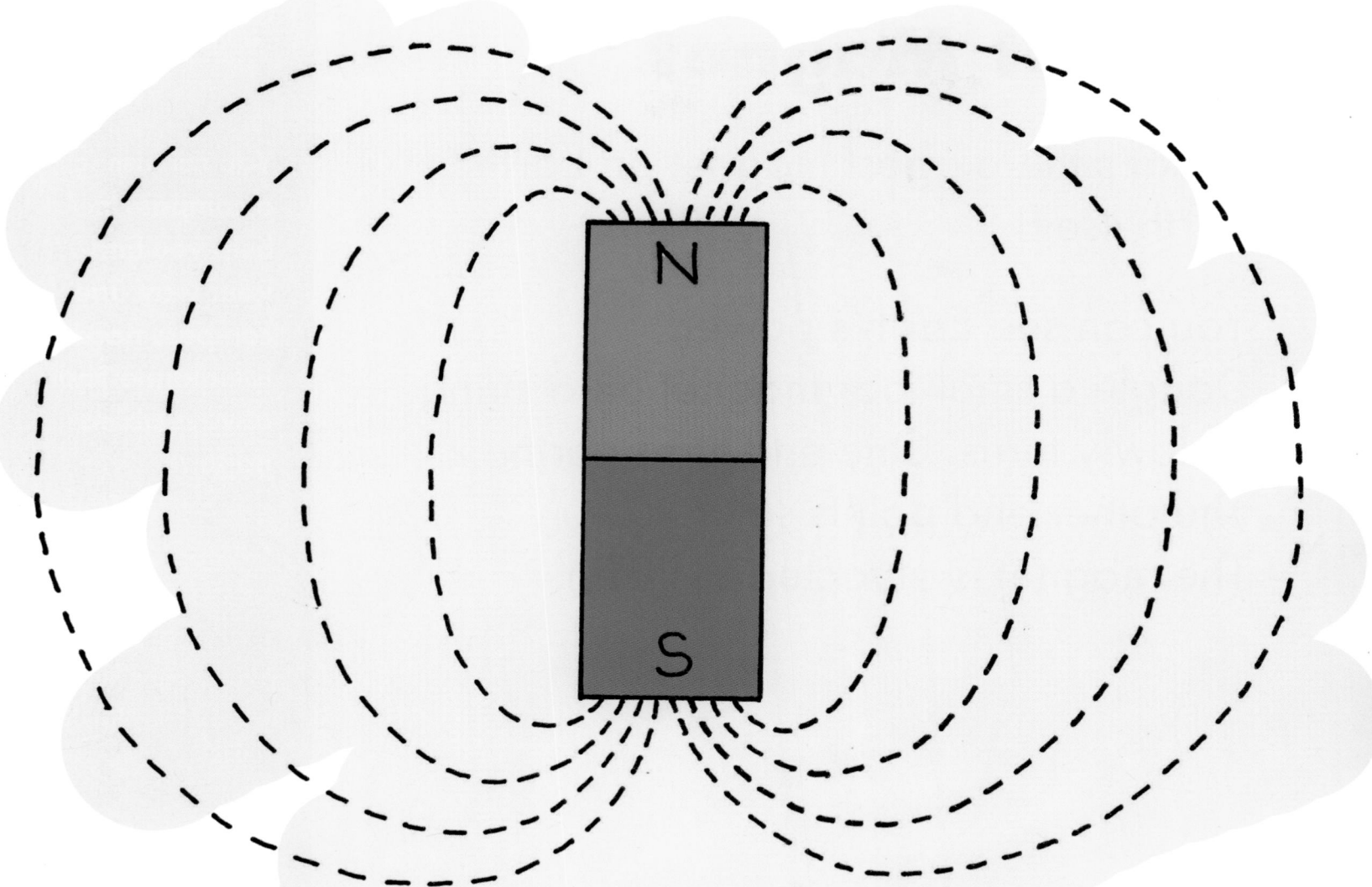

Planet Magnet

What's the biggest magnet on Earth?
Earth itself!

You can see Earth's power.
Dangle a small bar magnet on a string.
It slowly turns. One end turns north.
The other end points south.
The magnet is attracted to Earth.

You can use a compass to help you find your way. The compass needle is a magnet that always points north. ▶

14

The Power of Poles

A magnet's ends have special names. The one that is attracted to Earth's northern tip is called the north **pole**. The other end is the south pole.

A magnet's power is strongest at its poles. But it works only in certain ways.

A magnet's poles are marked with N and S. ▶

16

Line up two bar magnets like train cars.
Do the ends pull together?
If so, you've matched the north and
south poles. Opposite poles attract.

What if the ends push apart?
That means you've matched north
with north or south with south.
Poles that are alike **repel**.
They push each other apart.

The opposite poles on two magnets attract. ▶

These toy train cars are connected by magnets. If you turned the last car of this train around, it would not stick to the middle car. ▶

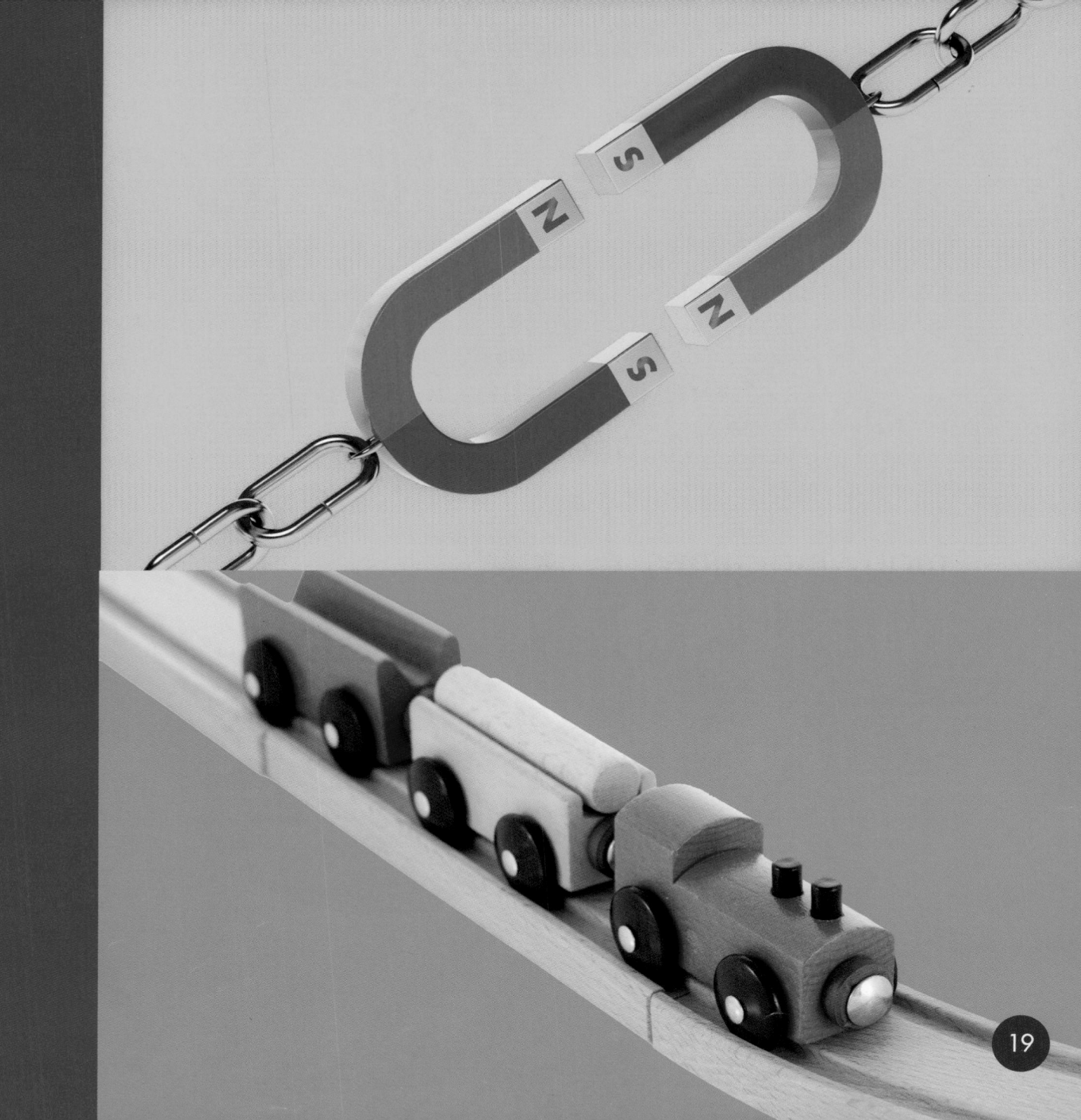

Magnets Every Day

Did you use a computer today?
Did you talk on the phone?
If so, you were using the power
of magnets. Magnets are
important parts of
many machines.

A telephone
uses magnets
to work. ▶

CD and DVD
players use
magnets, too! ◀

Many magnets are **electromagnets**.
Electricity makes them strong.
A powerful electromagnet can
pick up a car!

What else can magnets do?
Test it yourself with magnets!

More Magnet Magic

The door of your refrigerator is probably coated with plastic. But you can still use a magnet to stick artwork on it, right? That's because magnets can work through certain materials. Here's a list of a few things that let magnetic force through.

glass	cloth
air	plastic
paper	water

Words to Know

attract (uh-TRAKT): To attract is to pull together. Opposite poles on a magnet attract.

electromagnet (eh-LEK-tro-MAG-net): An electromagnet is a magnet that is made with electricity. An electromagnet can be very powerful.

magnetic (mag-NET-ik): Magnetic things will stick to a magnet. Magnetic objects most likely have a lot of iron in them.

magnetic field (mag-NET-ik FEELD): A magnetic field is the space around a magnet where the magnet works. The more powerful the magnet is, the stronger its magnetic field.

poles (POHLZ): Poles are ends of a magnet, where its power is strongest. One end is called the north pole, and the other is the south pole.

repel (ruh-PEHL): To repel is to push away. Alike poles on a magnet repel.